The INSIDE GUIDE

WOMEN IN U.S. HISTORY

Women of the Suffrage Movement

By Therese M. Shea

Cavendish Square

Published in 2025 by Cavendish Square Publishing, LLC
2544 Clinton Street Buffalo, NY 14224

First Edition

Cataloging-in-Publication Data

Names: Shea, Therese M.
Title: Women of the suffrage movement / Therese M. Shea
Description: Buffalo, NY : Cavendish Square Publishing, 2025. | Series: The inside guide: women in U.S. History | Includes glossary and index.
Identifiers: ISBN 9781502673145 (pbk.) | ISBN 9781502673152 (library bound) | ISBN 9781502673169 (ebook)
Subjects: LCSH: Women–Suffrage–History–20th century–United States–Juvenile literature. | Suffragists–United States–History.
Classification: LCC JF851.S48 2025 | DDC 324.6'2309730904–dc23

Editor: Therese Shea
Copyeditor: Danielle Haynes
Designer: Deanna Lepovich

The photographs in this book are used by permission and through the courtesy of: Cover Shutterstock AI Generator/ Shutterstock.com; p. 4 Drazen Zigic/Shutterstock.com; p. 6 courtesy of the National Archives; p. 7 Abigail Adams/Wikimedia Commons; p. 8 (top) John Singleton Copley - Portrait de Madame John Stevens/Wikimedia Commons; p. 8 (bottom) MaryWollstonecraft/ Wikimedia Commons; p. 8 (center) Vindication1b/Wikimedia Commons; p. 10 (main) Elizabeth Cady Stanton, 1889/Wikimedia Commons; p. 10 (inset) Mott Lucretia Painting Kyle 1841/Wikimedia Commons; p. 12 The Anti-Slavery Society Convention, 1840 by Benjamin Robert Haydon/Wikimedia Commons; p. 13 (right) Jane C Hunt of Seneca Falls/Wikimedia Commons; p. 13 (center) Martha C. Wright/Wikimedia Commons; p. 13 (left) Mary Ann M'Clintock/Wikimedia Commons; pp. 15 (top), 16, 20, 22, 23, 24, 25 courtesy of the Library of Congress; p. 15 (bottom) Women's Rights Convention attendees/Wikimedia Commons; p. 19 The House Joint Resolution Proposing the 15th Amendment to the Constitution, December 7, 1868; Enrolled Acts and Resolutions of Congress, 1789-1999; General Records of the United States Government; Record Group 11; National Archives; p. 21 Victoria C Woohull by Bradley & Rulofson (cropped)/Wikimedia Commons; p. 26 Joint Resolution of Congress proposing a constitutional amendment extending the right of suffrage to women, approved June 4, 1919.; Ratified Amendments, 1795-1992; General Records of the United States Government; Record Group 11; National Archives; p. 29 (left) Suffragists Parade Down Fifth Avenue, 1917/Wikimedia Commons; p. 29 (right) VOTE poster - Citation Acc 22002 - Archives and Manuscripts - Library of Virginia/Wikimedia Commons.

CPSIA compliance information: Batch #CWCSQ25: For further information contact Cavendish Square Publishing LLC at 1-877-980-4450.

Printed in the United States of America

CONTENTS

Suffrage is the right to vote in elections.

THE STRUGGLE FOR SUFFRAGE

Chapter One

The U.S. Constitution begins, "We the people." However, it didn't mean all people at first. The United States is a democracy, but nowhere in the original Constitution, the highest law in the country, did it say that all citizens have the right to vote. Instead, it gave states power over elections, including who can vote, reserving the right of Congress to overrule the states. Many elections left out large sections of the population, including women. It wasn't until more than 140 years after the nation's founding that all women were granted the right to vote, through the 19th **Amendment** to the Constitution.

Fast Fact

A democracy is a government in which the citizens have power. They make decisions through voting. The United States is an indirect democracy. People vote for representatives to make decisions in government.

Forgetting the Ladies

Women have been asking for more rights since the founding of the United States. Famously, Abigail Adams, the wife of Founding Father and second U.S. president John Adams, asked her husband to "remember the Ladies and be more

BRIEF SUFFRAGE IN NEW JERSEY

Women in the state of New Jersey could vote from the nation's beginning, for a few elections at least. In 1776, the New Jersey state constitution allowed anyone who had lived there for 12 months and who owned property to vote. This included Black New Jersey residents and single women, as long as they had property. (Married women couldn't own property; it was placed under their husband's care.) In 1790, the law was changed to use the words "he or she," which clearly gave the right to vote to women. However, in 1807, the state legislature limited voting to just white male citizens who paid taxes.

A part of Article I, Section 4 of the Constitution, which is shown here, says: "Times, Places and Manner of holding Elections for Senators and Representatives, shall be prescribed [directed] in each State by the Legislature thereof; but the Congress may at any time by Law make or alter such Regulations."

Abigail Adams, shown here, told her husband John in a 1776 letter that women might fight back if not given more rights: "[Women] will not hold ourselves bound by any Laws in which we have no voice, or Representation."

generous and favourable [good] to them than your ancestors," as he and other representatives worked to create a "new code of laws" for the new nation. She asked him not to "put such unlimited power into the hands of the Husbands."

John Adams wrote back, "We [Men] know better than to repeal [remove] our masculine [male] systems."

Fast Fact

In early U.S. history, married women had fewer rights than single women because of a legal standing called coverture. Married women were legally "covered" by their husbands. A married woman had no right to her own wealth or property, even if she brought it into the marriage.

In 1802, Judith Sargent Murray (*left*) and others opened a school for girls in Dorchester, Massachusetts. She recognized how women and men wouldn't be seen as equal until they had the same educational opportunities.

In 1790, writer Judith Sargent Murray argued for more rights in an essay called "On the Equality of the Sexes." Both Abigail Adams and Murray had advantages that many didn't,

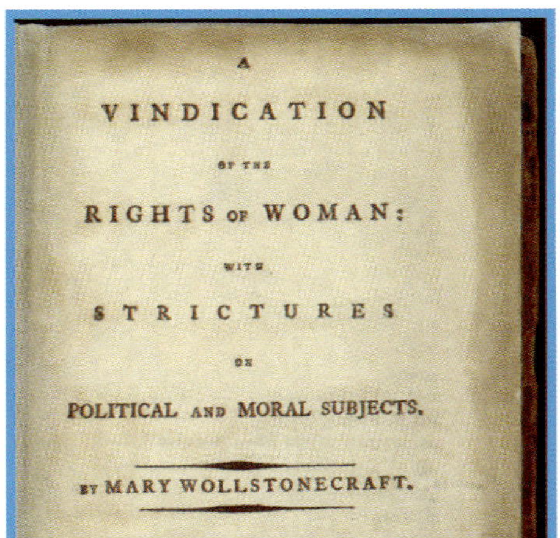

A
VINDICATION
OF THE
RIGHTS OF WOMAN:
WITH
STRICTURES
ON
POLITICAL AND MORAL SUBJECTS.
BY MARY WOLLSTONECRAFT.

PRINTED AT BOSTON,
BY PETER EDES FOR THOMAS AND ANDREWS,
FAUST's Statue, No. 45, Newbury-Street,
MDCCXCII.

Mary Wollstonecraft (*below*) was a British women's rights supporter who influenced the women's suffrage movement. She wrote a book arguing for equality called *A Vindication of the Rights of Woman*, published in 1792.

notably wealth and education. In those times, many girls weren't sent to school for long, if at all. Many didn't learn to read and write, especially if their family was poor. Instead, they learned from their mothers how to take care of a house and children because most women were expected to marry and become mothers, not pursue other jobs.

Slow to Change

At the end of the 18th century, laws regarding women's rights were changing—slowly. For example, women had gained a bit more control over the property they brought into their marriages in some places.

> **Fast Fact**
>
> In the early 1770s, the colonies of Maryland and New York passed laws that made sure husbands couldn't sell women's property without consulting them.

These were gains made primarily by white women, however. In the early 1800s, Black women held even fewer rights than white women. Enslaved women had no rights at all. In fact, the government considered them to be property.

Since women couldn't vote, they couldn't work through the government to gain more rights. They had to rely on men in government to work for their interests. More and more women came to realize how important suffrage was to their future.

Lucretia Mott (*upper right*) and Elizabeth Cady Stanton (*above*) played major roles in the U.S. women's suffrage movement.

THE CONVENTION

Chapter Two

The origins of the women's suffrage movement in the United States lie within the abolitionist movement, which was the organized fight to end slavery. Women played an important role in the abolitionist movement, but they weren't allowed to become members of the biggest abolitionist organization, the American Anti-Slavery Society, which was established in 1833. Lucretia Mott and about 20 other women formed their own abolitionist group called the Philadelphia Female Anti-Slavery Society. It invited both Black and white women to join, which wasn't common at the time.

A Fateful Meeting

In 1840, a **convention** was held in London, England, to discuss abolition. Some organizations sent women as delegates, or representatives, but most of the male delegates didn't want women to take part. Some said it was against British tradition or the Christian religion. It was finally decided that women delegates

> **Fast Fact**
>
> In the early 19th century, many states began extending voting rights to all white men, even if they didn't own property. Women were left out.

Fast Fact

The book *History of Woman Suffrage, Volume 1*, cowritten by Elizabeth Cady Stanton, says, "The movement for woman's suffrage, both in England and America, may be dated from the World's Anti-Slavery Convention."

While this painting of the 1840 London antislavery convention shows men and women together, women weren't invited to be active participants.

could listen behind a curtain but couldn't speak to the assembly as male delegates could.

Two of the women present, Lucretia Mott and Elizabeth Cady Stanton, who were both abolitionists, met at this convention. The male delegates' actions inspired Mott and Stanton to talk about how to work toward more women's rights. They decided to hold a convention when they returned to the United States.

What Happened in Seneca Falls

Eight years later, in 1848, the Women's Rights Convention, later called the Seneca Falls Convention, took place from July 19 to 20 in Seneca Falls, New York, the home of Elizabeth Cady Stanton. About 300 people attended, mostly from nearby areas.

On the convention's first day, Stanton read the Declaration of Sentiments, which was a statement of injustices and demands written

Three lesser-known organizers of the Seneca Falls Convention were Mary Ann M'Clintock (*left*), who cofounded the Philadelphia Female Anti-Slavery Society; Martha Coffin Wright (*middle*), Lucretia Mott's sister; and Jane Hunt (*right*), who was related to M'Clintock.

THE OPENING SPEECH

Elizabeth Cady Stanton, one of the Seneca Falls Convention's chief organizers, opened the meeting by stating its purpose:

> *We are assembled to protest against a form of government, existing without the consent of the governed—to declare our right to be free as man is free, to be represented in the government which we are taxed to support, to have such disgraceful laws as give man the power to* ***chastise*** *and imprison his wife, to take the wages which she earns, the property which she inherits, and, in case of separation, the children of her love ... if possible, forever erased.*

Fast Fact

Men were asked not to attend the first day of the Seneca Falls Convention.

to sound like the Declaration of Independence. Then, the convention discussed 11 resolutions on women's rights. One of these resolutions stated that laws that held women as inferior, or less than, men were against nature and had "no force or authority." Another resolution said women should be able to preach in religious assemblies as men could.

Ten resolutions passed unanimously, or with complete agreement. The only one that didn't pass unanimously was that women should have "the elective franchise," or the right to vote. Mott believed it didn't receive as much support because some thought they might be asking too much and that others wouldn't help their

Frederick Douglass escaped enslavement in 1838 and became a leader in the abolitionist movement. He was a powerful public speaker who was widely respected.

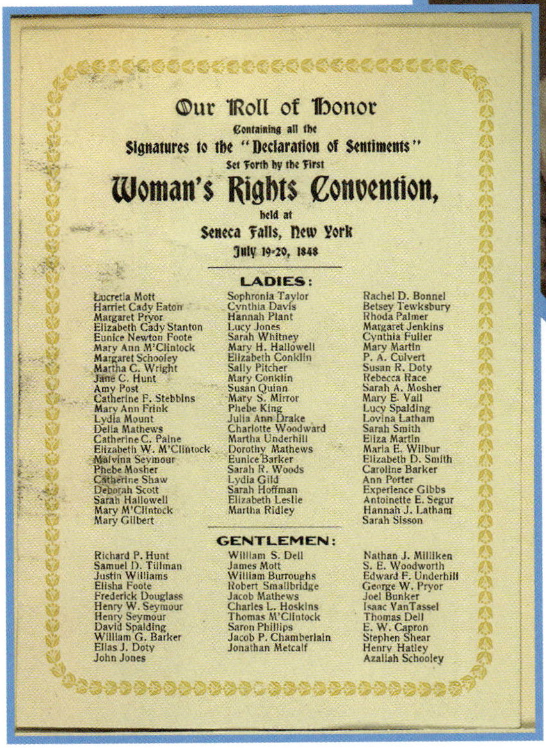

Our Roll of Honor

Containing all the

Signatures to the "Declaration of Sentiments"

Set Forth by the First

Woman's Rights Convention,

held at

Seneca Falls, New York

July 19-20, 1848

LADIES:

Lucretia Mott
Harriet Cady Eaton
Margaret Pryor
Elizabeth Cady Stanton
Eunice Newton Foote
Mary Ann M'Clintock
Margaret Schooley
Martha C. Wright
Jane C. Hunt
Amy Post
Catherine F. Stebbins
Mary Ann Frink
Lydia Mount
Delia Mathews
Catherine C. Paine
Elizabeth W. M'Clintock
Malvina Seymour
Phebe Mosher
Catherine Shaw
Deborah Scott
Sarah Hallowell
Mary M'Clintock
Mary Gilbert
Sophronia Taylor
Cynthia Davis
Hannah Plant
Lucy Jones
Sarah Whitney
Mary H. Hallowell
Elizabeth Conklin
Sally Pitcher
Mary Conklin
Susan Quinn
Mary S. Mirror
Phebe King
Julia Ann Drake
Charlotte Woodward
Martha Underhill
Dorothy Mathews
Eunice Barker
Sarah R. Woods
Lydia Gild
Sarah Hoffman
Elizabeth Leslie
Martha Ridley
Rachel D. Bonnel
Betsey Tewksbury
Rhoda Palmer
Margaret Jenkins
Cynthia Fuller
Mary Martin
P. A. Culvert
Susan R. Doty
Rebecca Race
Sarah A. Mosher
Mary E. Vail
Lucy Spalding
Lovina Latham
Sarah Smith
Eliza Martin
Maria E. Wilbur
Elizabeth D. Smith
Caroline Barker
Ann Porter
Experience Gibbs
Antoinette E. Segur
Hannah J. Latham
Sarah Sisson

GENTLEMEN:

Richard P. Hunt
Samuel D. Tillman
Justin Williams
Elisha Foote
Frederick Douglass
Henry W. Seymour
Henry Seymour
David Spalding
William G. Barker
Elias J. Doty
John Jones
William S. Dell
James Mott
William Burroughs
Robert Smallbridge
Jacob Mathews
Charles L. Hoskins
Thomas M'Clintock
Saron Phillips
Jacob P. Chamberlain
Jonathan Metcalf
Nathan J. Milliken
S. E. Woodworth
Edward F. Underhill
George W. Pryor
Joel Bunker
Isaac VanTassel
Thomas Dell
E. W. Capron
Stephen Shear
Henry Hatley
Azaliah Schooley

These are the names of the men and women who signed the Declaration of Sentiments at the Seneca Falls Convention in 1848.

efforts if they pursued the right to vote.

Stanton spoke powerfully for the right to vote as did Black abolitionist and women's rights supporter Frederick Douglass. Because of their words, which reasoned that the right to vote could help secure all other rights, the resolution passed with a small majority.

Sojourner Truth was a powerful champion for women's rights, abolition, and temperance.

Chapter Three

ORGANIZING AND INCREASING SUPPORT

In October 1850, the National Women's Rights Convention was held in Worcester, Massachusetts. About 1,000 people attended from a wider area than those who had attended the Seneca Falls Convention two years before. Organized by the suffragist, or supporter of women's suffrage, Lucy Stone, the convention received attention in the international press. Lucretia Mott, Sojourner Truth, writer Ralph Waldo Emerson, and abolitionist William Lloyd Garrison were among those who attended.

A Split

At first, many in the suffrage movement thought the best way to gain the vote was for each state to amend its constitution. Women spoke in front of state legislatures, asking for suffrage. Some men and women who didn't support the suffrage movement spoke too.

> **Fast Fact**
>
> Sometimes people who were against women's rights attended the conventions so they could disrupt them.

The movement slowed when the American Civil War began in

SOJOURNER SPEAKS THE TRUTH

Sojourner Truth, an abolitionist and formerly enslaved woman, spoke at an 1851 women's rights convention in Akron, Ohio. In a famous speech, now called "Ain't I a Woman?," she challenged **stereotypes** of weak women who needed men to help them. She spoke as an American woman and as a Black woman. She said she could do as much work as any man and no man had to come to her rescue. Some historians suggest her words and how she said them might have been changed in later accounts of her speech. However, by all accounts, the crowd thought she was engaging, funny, and powerful. Truth spoke at many more conventions.

1861. Many suffragists were abolitionists, so they supported the war effort, which would bring an end to slavery in the United States. After the war, in 1869, the U.S. Congress passed the 15th Amendment to the Constitution, which gave Black men the right to vote, but 28 state legislatures still needed to approve it for it to become law.

The 15th Amendment split the suffrage movement. Some, such as Lucy Stone, supported the amendment, believing it was important to grant the vote to Black men immediately. Others, such as Elizabeth Cady Stanton and Susan B. Anthony, were against it because it didn't also give women the right to vote.

In 1869, Stanton and Anthony founded the National Woman Suffrage Association (NWSA), and Stone founded the American

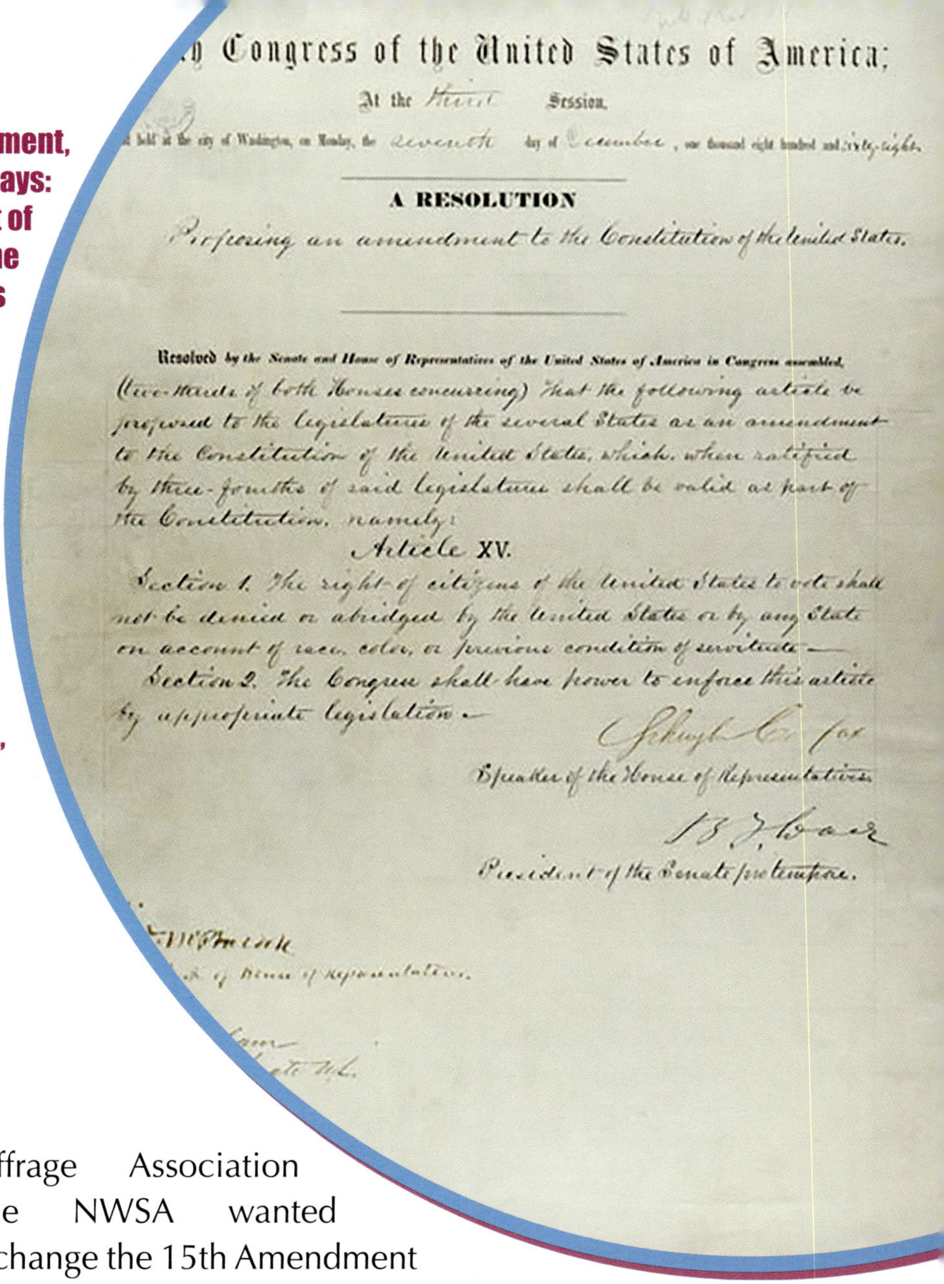
Congress of the United States of America;

At the third Session,

held at the city of Washington, on Monday, the seventh day of December, one thousand eight hundred and sixty-eight.

A RESOLUTION

Proposing an amendment to the Constitution of the United States.

Resolved by the Senate and House of Representatives of the United States of America in Congress assembled, (two-thirds of both Houses concurring) That the following article be proposed to the legislatures of the several States as an amendment to the Constitution of the United States, which, when ratified by three-fourths of said legislatures shall be valid as part of the Constitution, namely:

Article XV.

Section 1. The right of citizens of the United States to vote shall not be denied or abridged by the United States or by any State on account of race, color, or previous condition of servitude—

Section 2. The Congress shall have power to enforce this article by appropriate legislation—

Speaker of the House of Representatives.

President of the Senate pro tempore.

The 15th Amendment, shown here, says: "The right of citizens of the United States to vote shall not be denied or abridged [lessened] by the United States or by any State on account of race, color, or previous condition of servitude."

Woman Suffrage Association (AWSA). The NWSA wanted lawmakers to change the 15th Amendment to include women. The AWSA, which supported the 15th Amendment as it was, focused on getting women the right to vote in local and state elections. The 15th Amendment was ratified, or officially approved, on February 3, 1870, without including language supporting women's suffrage.

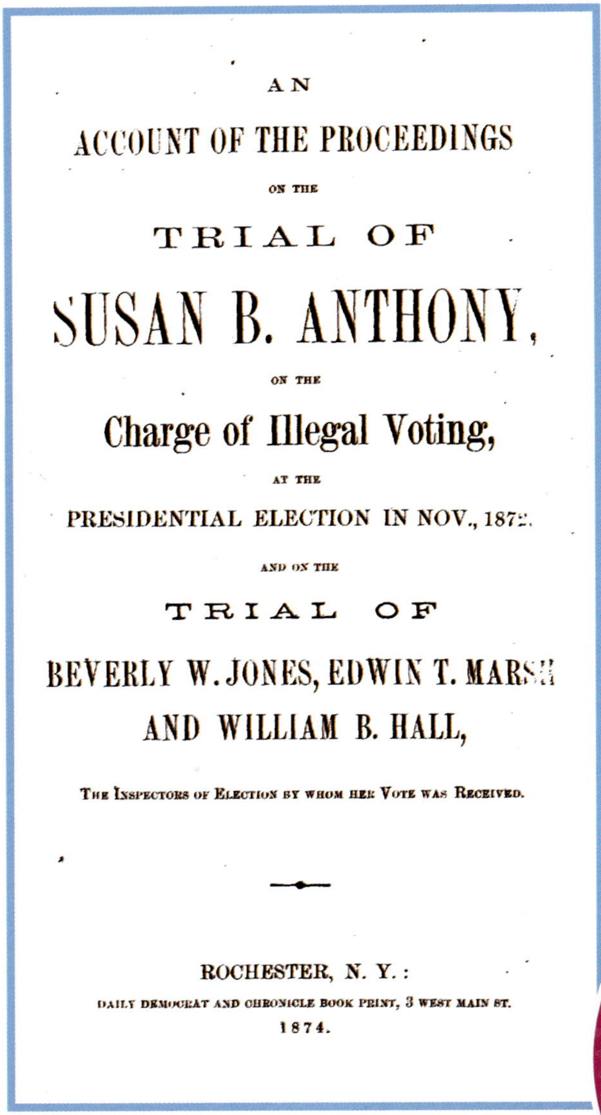

AN
ACCOUNT OF THE PROCEEDINGS
ON THE
TRIAL OF
SUSAN B. ANTHONY,
ON THE
Charge of Illegal Voting,
AT THE
PRESIDENTIAL ELECTION IN NOV., 1872,
AND ON THE
TRIAL OF
BEVERLY W. JONES, EDWIN T. MARSH
AND WILLIAM B. HALL,
THE INSPECTORS OF ELECTION BY WHOM HER VOTE WAS RECEIVED.

ROCHESTER, N. Y.:
DAILY DEMOCRAT AND CHRONICLE BOOK PRINT, 3 WEST MAIN ST.
1874.

In a new tactic, several women voted in the presidential election of 1872, hoping to use the legal system to argue for suffrage. Susan B. Anthony was arrested for voting in New York, as shown above. She argued for her right to vote in court but was found guilty.

Together Again

The NWSA and AWSA came together in 1890 to form the National American Woman Suffrage Association (NAWSA). The organization had a new plan: to persuade enough state legislatures to grant women the right to vote that the U.S. government would be forced to approve a new amendment to the U.S. Constitution granting women suffrage.

Between 1890 and 1896, Wyoming, Colorado, Utah,

Fast Fact

The first nation in the world to grant women the right to vote was New Zealand, in 1893.

Fast Fact

In 1869, the Wyoming Territory gave women the right to vote. When it became a state in 1890, its constitution was the first to give women suffrage. Wyoming is called the Equality State.

In 1872, Victoria Woodhull became the first woman to run for U.S. president. She was the candidate for the Equal Rights Party (though she was too young, at 34, to become president).

and Idaho became the first four states to give women the right to vote. However, no new states would include women's suffrage in their constitutions until Washington in 1910.

Into the 20th century, the suffrage movement still faced opposition, but more and more Americans began to support women's right to vote.

Chapter Four

TO THE FINISH LINE

In the early 1900s, some members of the NAWSA sought a more **aggressive** way of getting the vote. Alice Paul, head of the NAWSA Washington, D.C., branch, led marches and protests. Paul helped organize more than 5,000 women to march from the U.S. Capitol to the White House in 1913, one day before Woodrow Wilson was sworn in as U.S. president. Wilson said it wasn't yet time for a suffrage amendment.

The suffrage march of 1913 was met with some support from onlookers but also some violence. Some marchers were shouted at and even attacked.

Fast Fact

Alice Paul founded the Congressional Union for Woman Suffrage in 1913 to focus on a federal constitutional amendment. It later became the National Woman's Party.

Black Suffragists

The 1913 march highlighted a serious problem with the suffrage movement—**racism**. Black suffragists arrived to march with their delegations and were told to walk in the back of the parade. Some, including Ida B. Wells and Mary Church Terrell, refused to follow these instructions.

The NAWSA welcomed Black members at the national level, but state and local NAWSA groups sometimes didn't, or they **segregated** members. Black

Fast Fact

Black suffragist Adella Hunt Logan wrote in *The Crisis*, the magazine of the National Association for the Advancement of Colored People (NAACP), that Black women needed to vote even more than white women because they faced both sexism and racism.

Nannie Helen Burroughs is shown here holding a Woman's National Baptist Convention banner. She founded several groups to fight for the rights of Black people.

reformers' concerns were often ignored by the national organization, so they had begun their own organizations to support suffrage and other important causes for Black communities, such as laws to combat **lynching**. Terrell and Nannie Helen Burroughs founded the National Association of Colored Women in 1896.

The Push to Amend

In 1916, the NAWSA, led by Carrie Chapman Catt, introduced what was called its "Winning Plan." NAWSA efforts shifted to arguing for both a federal constitutional amendment and state constitutional amendments. New York adopted a woman's suffrage amendment in 1917.

The National Woman's Party staged the first-ever White House **picket**, in 1917. For months, women stood at the White House in silence six days a week. Some, including Alice Paul and Lucy Burns, were arrested for blocking traffic. In jail, Paul, Burns,

Women represent the colleges they attended as they picket the White House in February 1917 in support of women's suffrage.

and others started a hunger strike. These actions gained sympathy for the suffrage movement.

In 1918, President Woodrow Wilson finally gave his support to women's suffrage. The major political parties followed. By June 1919, Congress had passed the 19th Amendment to the Constitution, guaranteeing U.S. women the right to vote. By August 1920, two-thirds of the state legislatures had approved it as well, making it law.

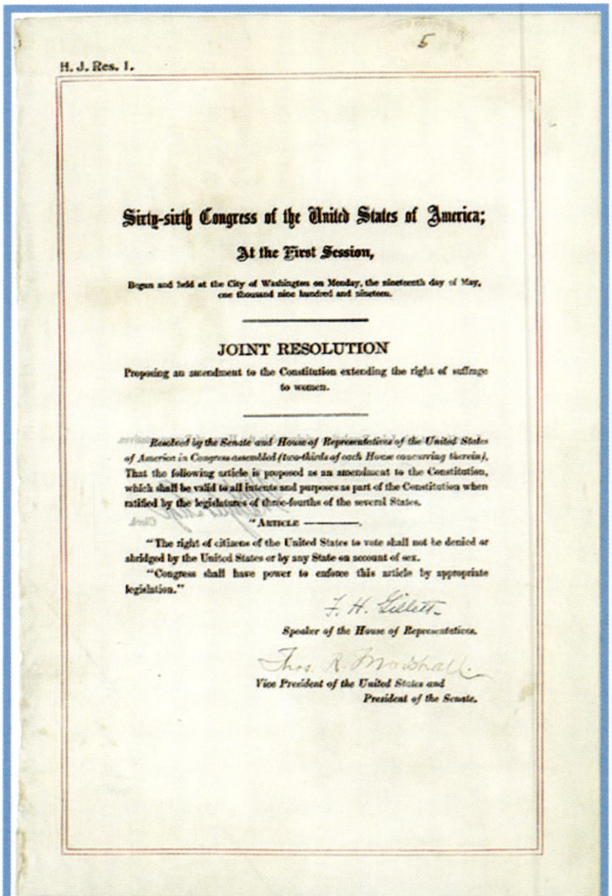

H. J. Res. 1.

Sixty-sixth Congress of the United States of America;

At the First Session,

Begun and held at the City of Washington on Monday, the nineteenth day of May, one thousand nine hundred and nineteen.

JOINT RESOLUTION

Proposing an amendment to the Constitution extending the right of suffrage to women.

Resolved by the Senate and House of Representatives of the United States of America in Congress assembled (two-thirds of each House concurring therein), That the following article is proposed as an amendment to the Constitution, which shall be valid to all intents and purposes as part of the Constitution when ratified by the legislatures of three-fourths of the several States.

"ARTICLE ——.

"The right of citizens of the United States to vote shall not be denied or abridged by the United States or by any State on account of sex.

"Congress shall have power to enforce this article by appropriate legislation."

F. H. Gillett

Speaker of the House of Representatives.

Thos. R. Marshall

Vice President of the United States and President of the Senate.

The 19th Amendment, which is shown here, was first introduced to Congress in 1878. Finally approved in 1920, it says: "The right of citizens of the United States to vote shall not be denied or abridged by the United States or by any State on account of sex."

Not the End

In a speech at the White House after the passage of the 19th Amendment, Carrie Chapman Catt said to women, "That vote has been costly. Prize it. The vote is a power, a weapon of offense and defense, a prayer. Use it intelligently, **conscientiously**, prayerfully. Progress is calling to you to make no pause. Act."

Women won the right to vote, but the struggle for equal rights wasn't over.

NATIVE AMERICAN SUFFRAGE

Many Native American women had long experienced equality in their own Native nations. For example, Haudenosaunee (Iroquois) women were "the great power among the clan," as described by Elizabeth Cady Stanton. Women chose the clan chiefs and removed them too. These customs and others inspired women of the U.S. suffrage movement. Native Americans were granted U.S. citizenship in 1924, through the Snyder Act, so they should have been able to vote. However, many faced the same obstacles Black Americans faced. States made them take tests, pay taxes, or face other challenges before they could vote. Later legislation finally removed these barriers.

Fast Fact

Before the Voting Rights Act, literacy tests kept many Americans from voting, including Spanish-speaking Puerto Ricans, who couldn't pass the tests in English.

Many women and men, especially Black Americans in the South, were kept from voting by state laws that set up obstacles such as voting, or poll, taxes and **literacy** requirements. However, people kept fighting for their rights.

The Voting Rights Act of 1965 removed these voting obstacles, but rulings by the U.S. Supreme Court in the 21st century have weakened this act and allowed for new obstacles to make it harder for certain groups to vote. The fight for all the people of the United States to exercise their right to vote continues to this day, and women continue to be on the front lines of this fight.

A TIMELINE OF THE AMERICAN SUFFRAGE MOVEMENT

1848
Elizabeth Cady Stanton, Lucretia Mott, and others organize a women's rights convention in Seneca Falls, New York.

1850
The first national women's rights convention takes place in Worcester, Massachusetts.

1851
Sojourner Truth delivers her famous speech, "Ain't I a Woman?," at a women's rights convention in Akron, Ohio.

1869
The National Woman Suffrage Association (NWSA) and the American Woman Suffrage Association (AWSA) are founded.

1872
Victoria Woodhull runs for president. Susan B. Anthony votes in the presidential election and is arrested.

1890
The NWSA and AWSA combine to form the largest women's suffrage organization, the National American Woman Suffrage Association (NAWSA).

1896
Mary Church Terrell and Nannie Helen Burroughs found the National Association of Colored Women.

1913
Alice Paul, Lucy Burns, and thousands of women march for suffrage in Washington, D.C.

1916
Carrie Chapman Catt introduces the NAWSA's "Winning Plan."

1917
Alice Paul and the National Woman's Party begin to picket the White House.

1919
Congress passes the 19th Amendment.

1920
The 19th Amendment is passed by two-thirds of state legislatures and becomes law, granting women the right to vote.

THINK ABOUT IT!

1. How might the women's suffrage movement have been different if Elizabeth Cady Stanton and Lucretia Mott had been allowed to speak at the World Anti-Slavery Convention in 1840?
2. Why do you think so many suffragists were also abolitionists?
3. Why do you think some men and women didn't support suffrage?
4. Which do you think were the most effective tactics to gain the right to vote, and why?

GLOSSARY

aggressive: Acting with forceful energy and determination.

amendment: A change or addition to a constitution.

chastise: To punish or criticize.

conscientiously: In a careful or moral way.

convention: A gathering of people who have a common interest or purpose.

disrupt: To try to upset or inject disorder.

literacy: The ability to read and write.

lynch: Often done by a mob, to kill someone illegally for a supposed crime.

picket: A method of protest in which people stand outside a certain place and try to persuade others not to enter it.

racism: The practice of treating others poorly because they are part of a different race, or group of people who look alike in certain ways. This word also relates to governments and societies that allow one race to be treated better than others.

segregate: To forcefully separate races or classes.

stereotype: An often unfair and untrue belief people have about all members of a certain group.

tactic: A method for accomplishing a goal.

temperance: The practice or idea of drinking little to no alcohol.

FIND OUT MORE

Books

Harts, Shannon H. *Susan B. Anthony and Elizabeth Cady Stanton*. New York, NY: Gareth Stevens Publishing, 2022.

Stanborough, Rebecca. *A Women's Suffrage Time Capsule: Artifacts of the Movement for Voting Rights*. North Mankato, MN: Capstone Press, 2021.

Tyner, Artika R. *Focus on the Women's Suffrage Movement*. Minneapolis, MN: Lerner Publications, 2023.

Websites

Seneca Falls Resolutions: Women's Rights Demands in 1848
www.thoughtco.com/seneca-falls-resolutions-3530486
Read all 11 resolutions that were approved at the Seneca Falls Convention.

20 Suffragists to Know
www.nps.gov/subjects/womenshistory/20-for-2020.htm
Read biographies of these important activists.

The Women's Suffrage Movement
kids.nationalgeographic.com/history/article/womens-suffrage-movement
Review the historical events that led to the 19th Amendment.

INDEX